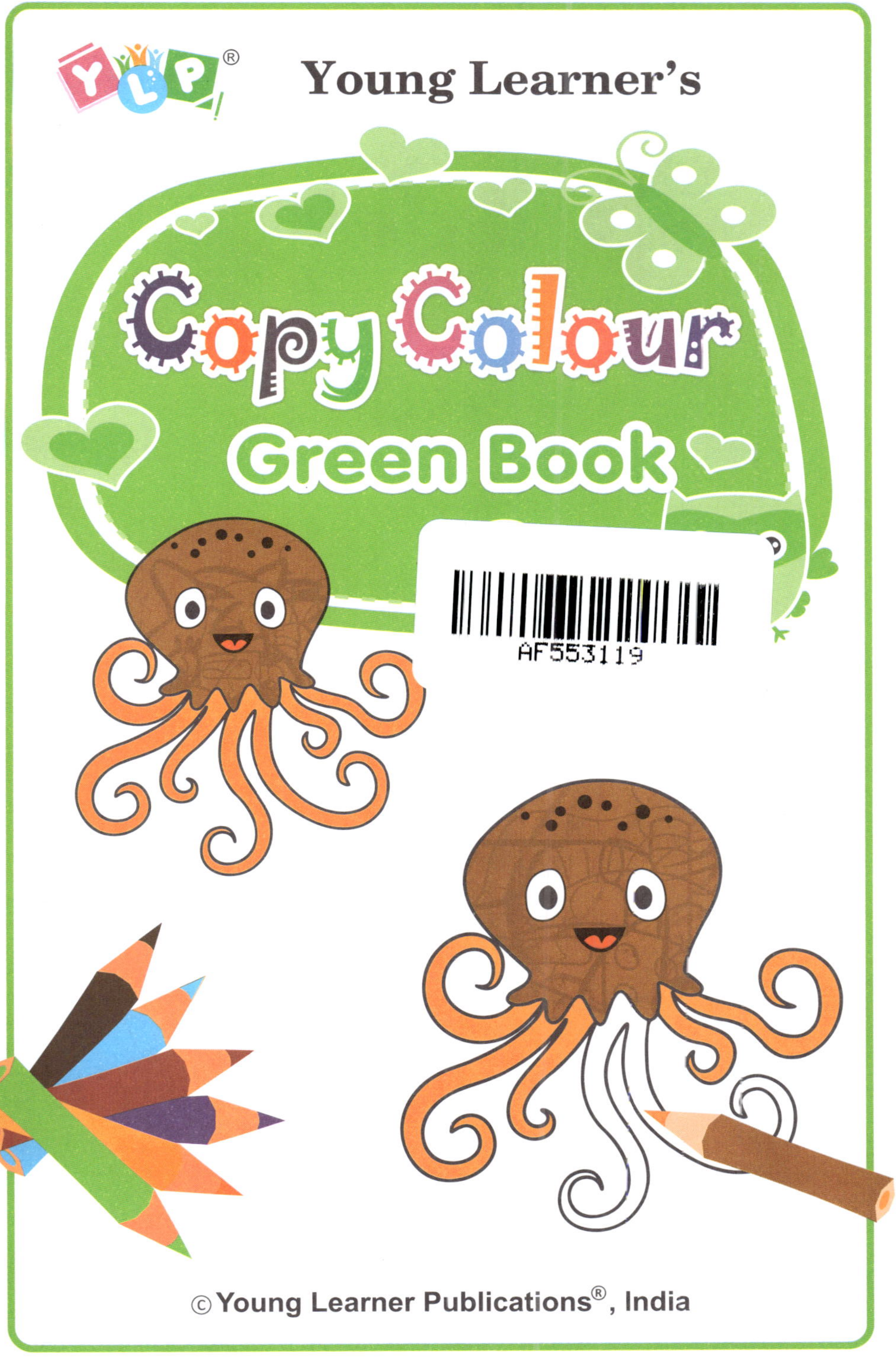
YLP
Young Learner's
Copy Colour
Green Book
AF553119

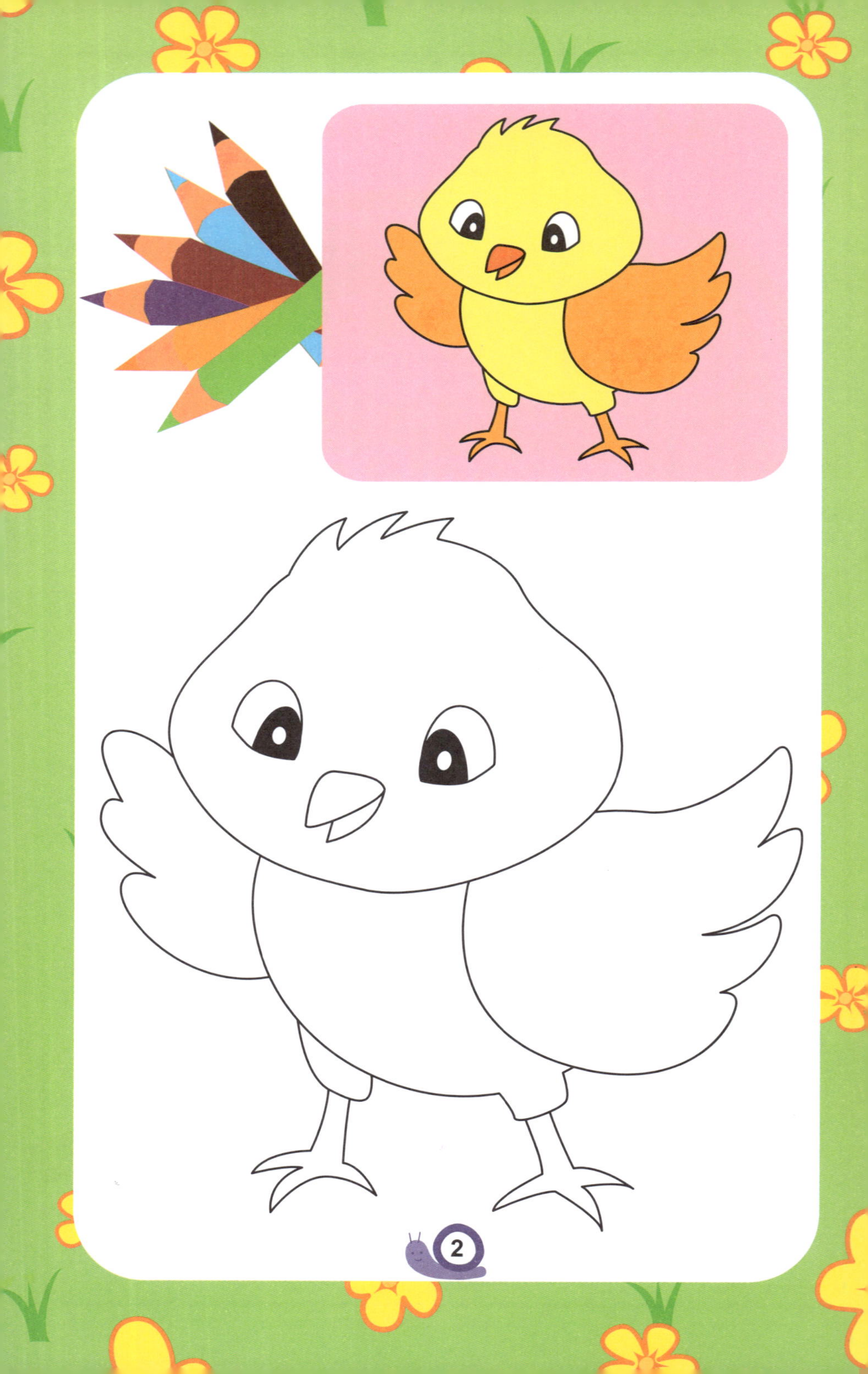

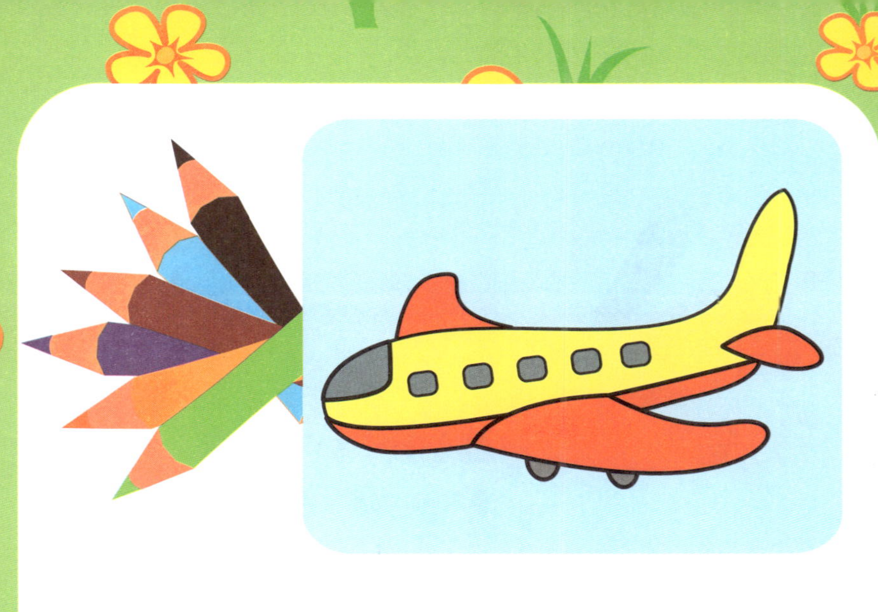

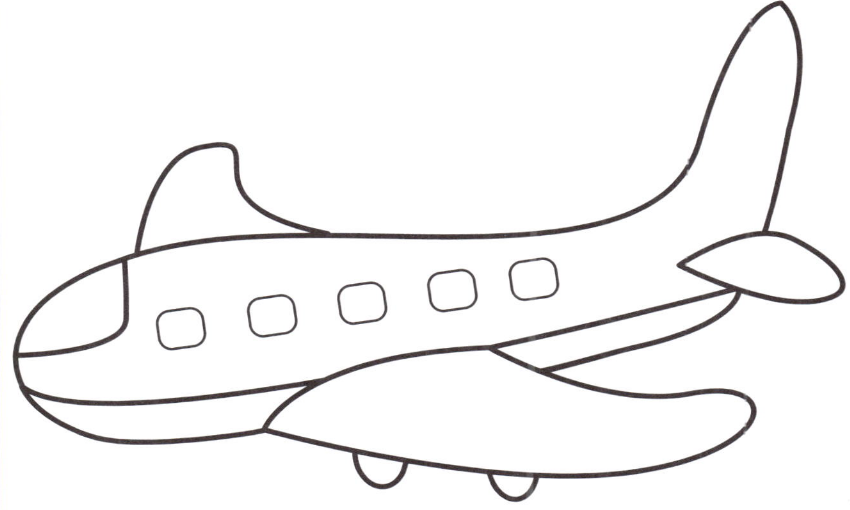

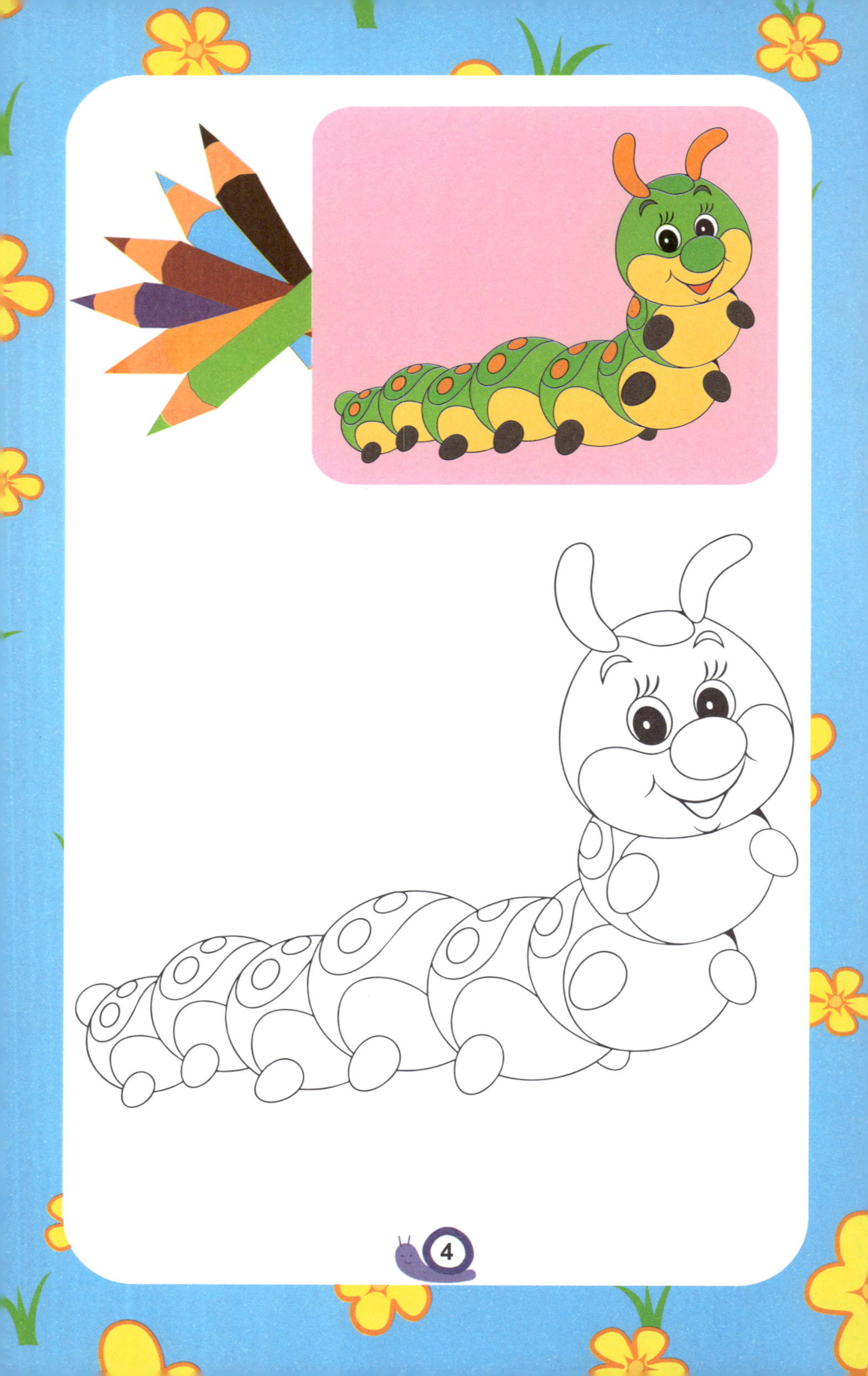

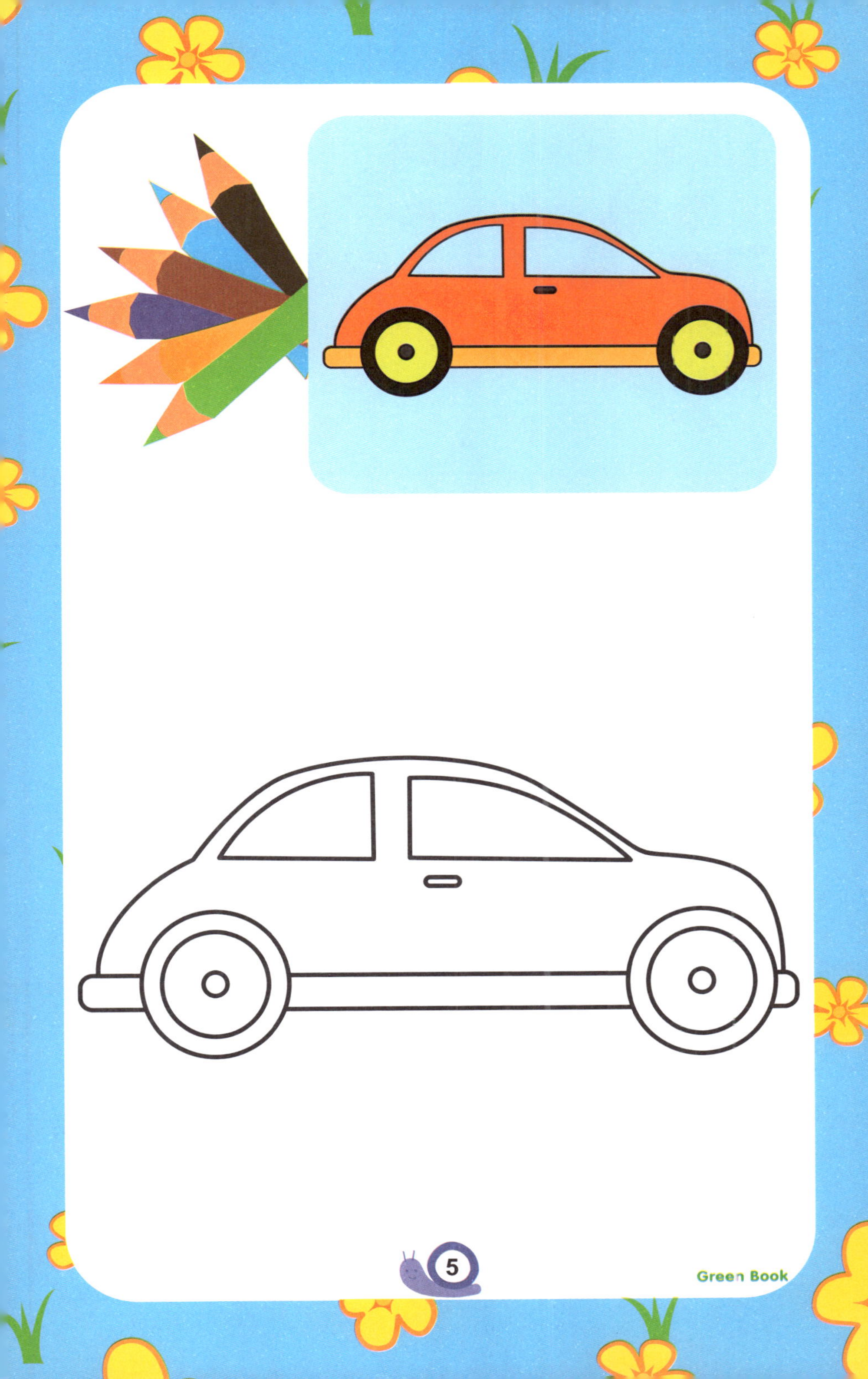

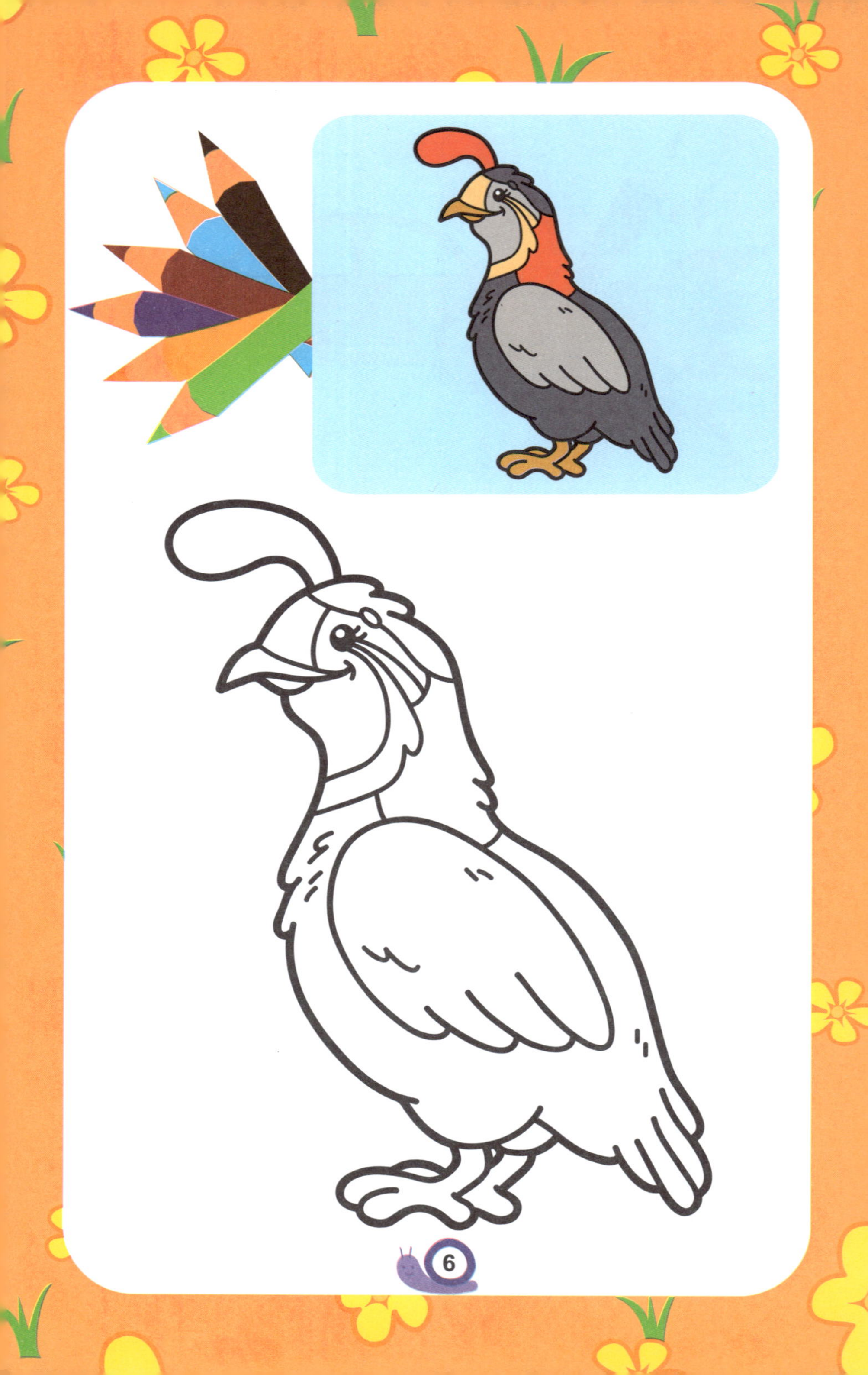

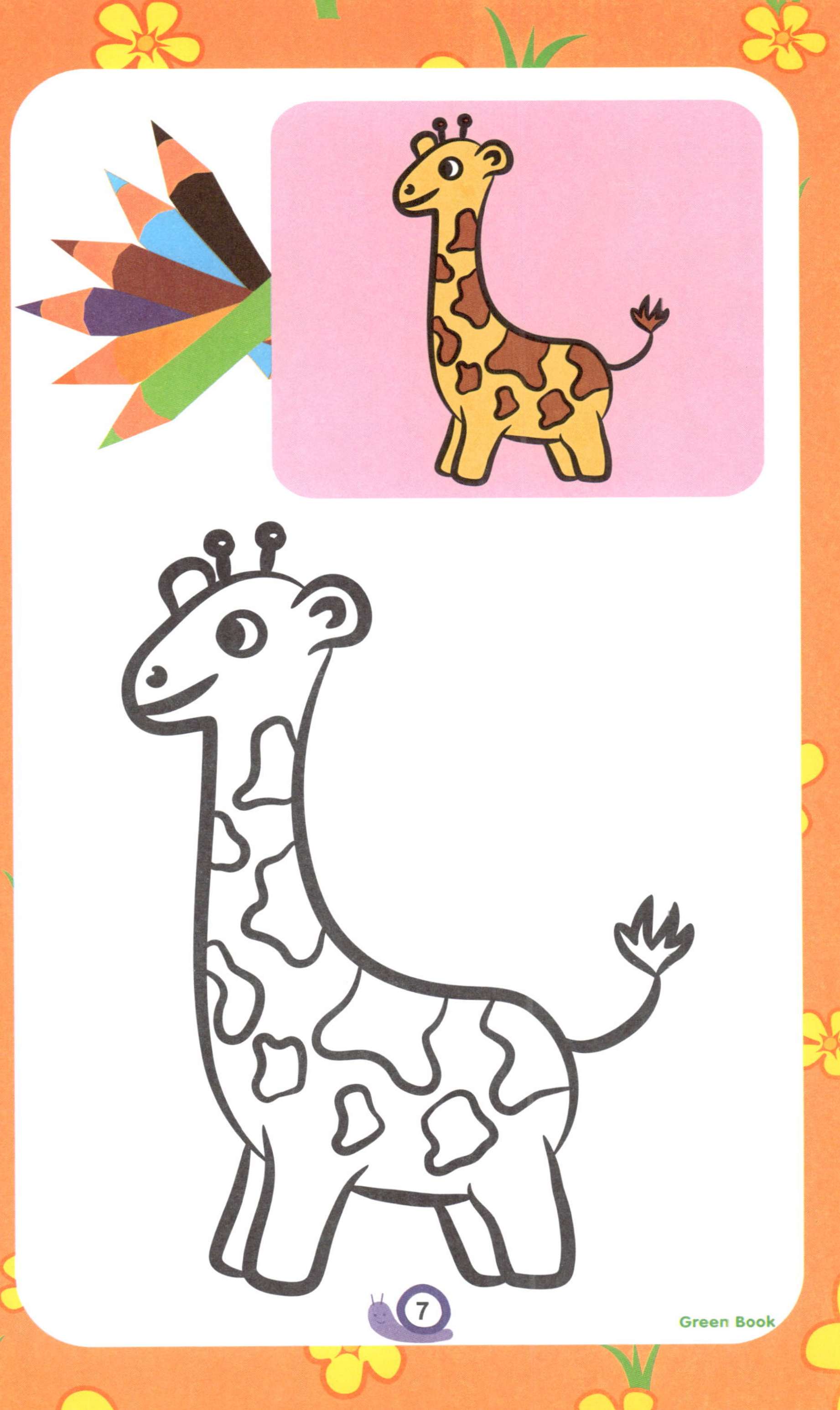

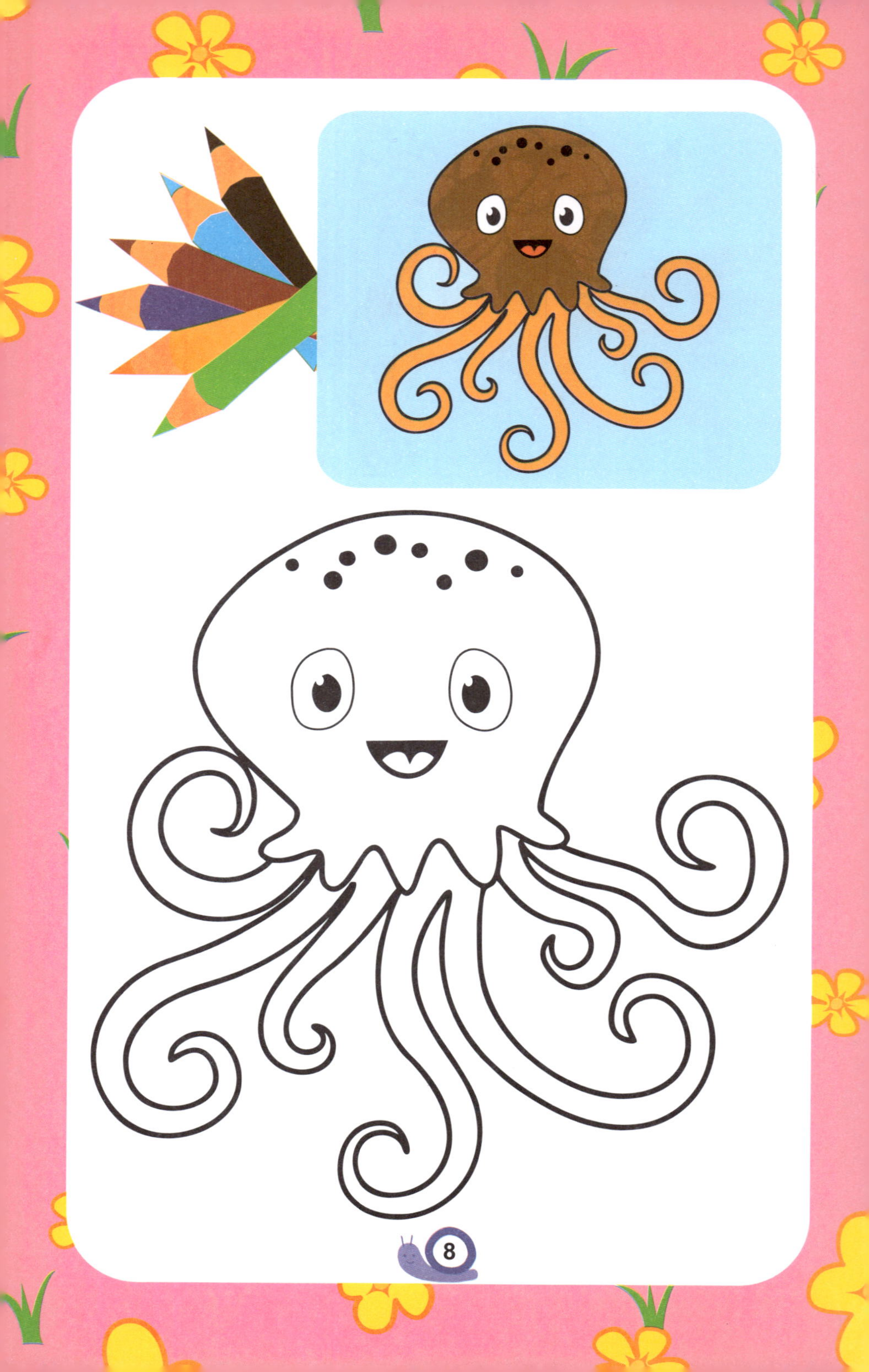

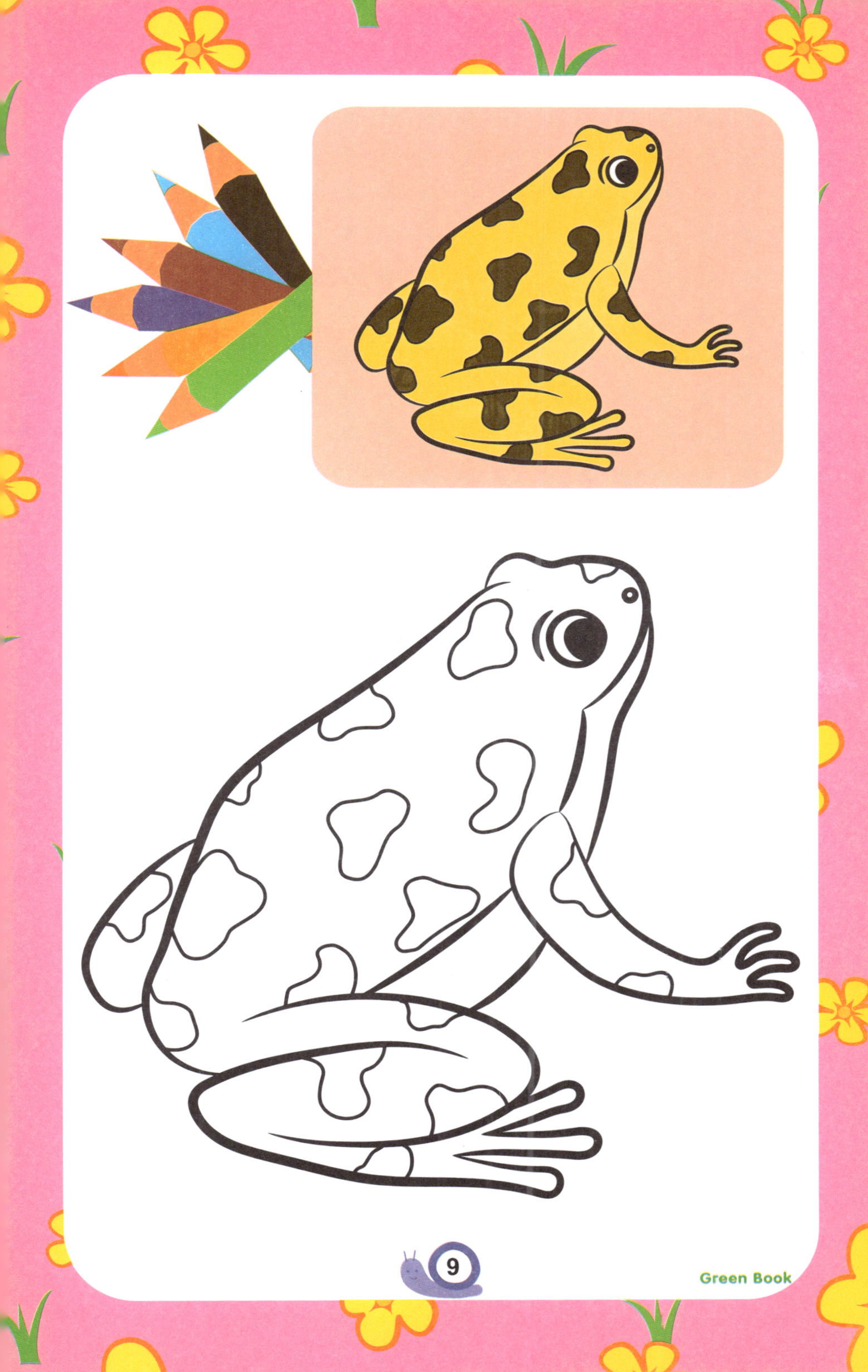

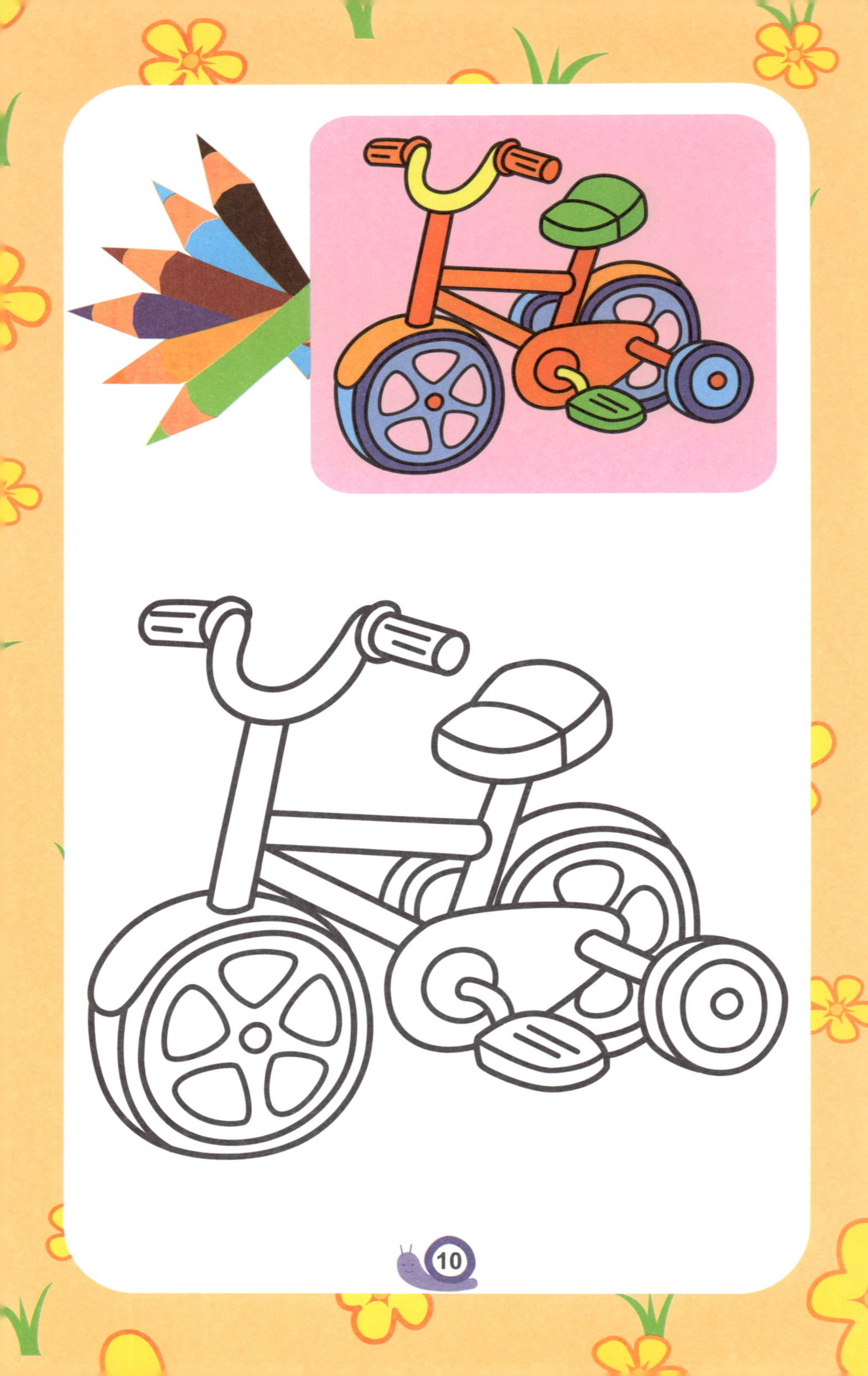

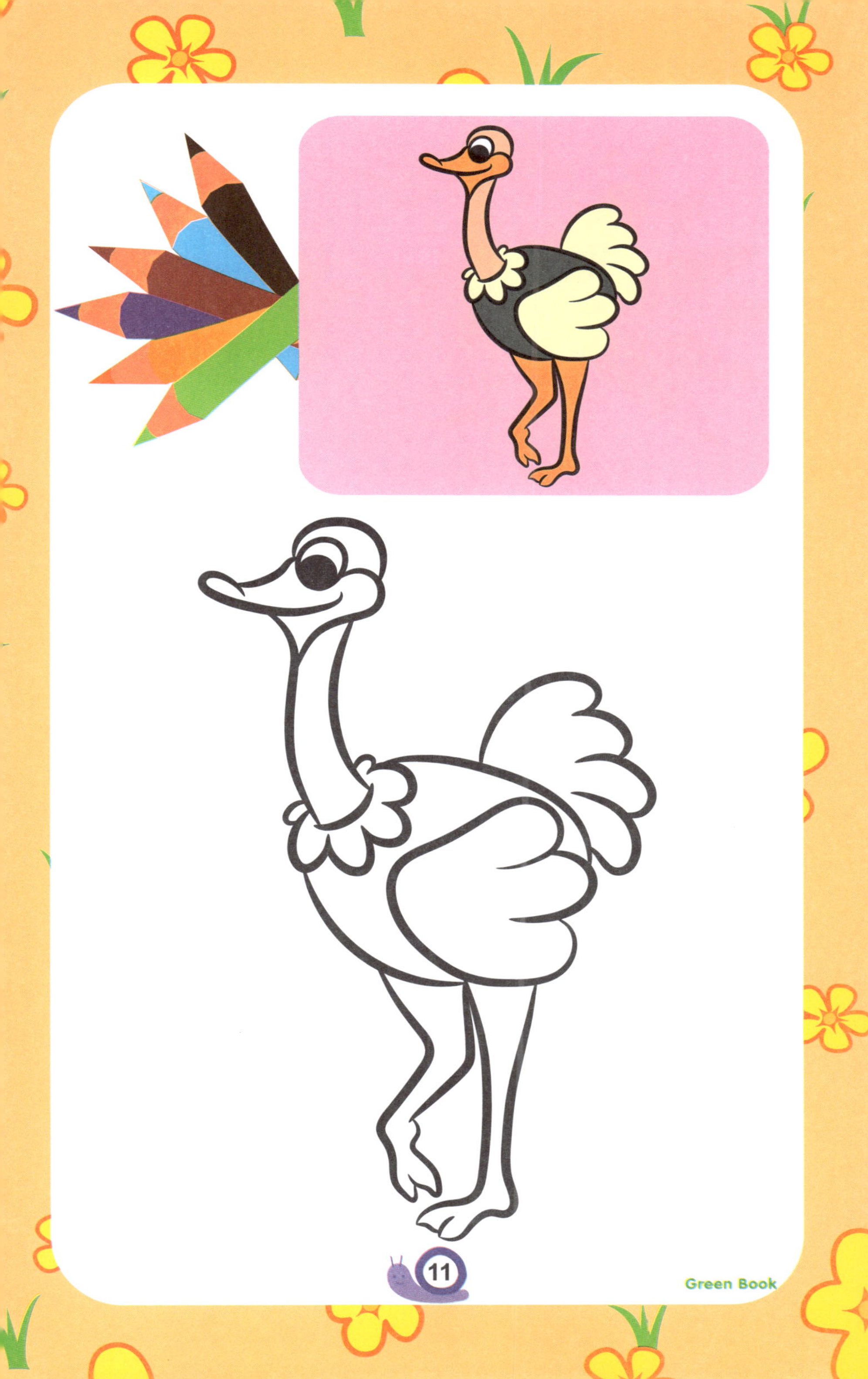

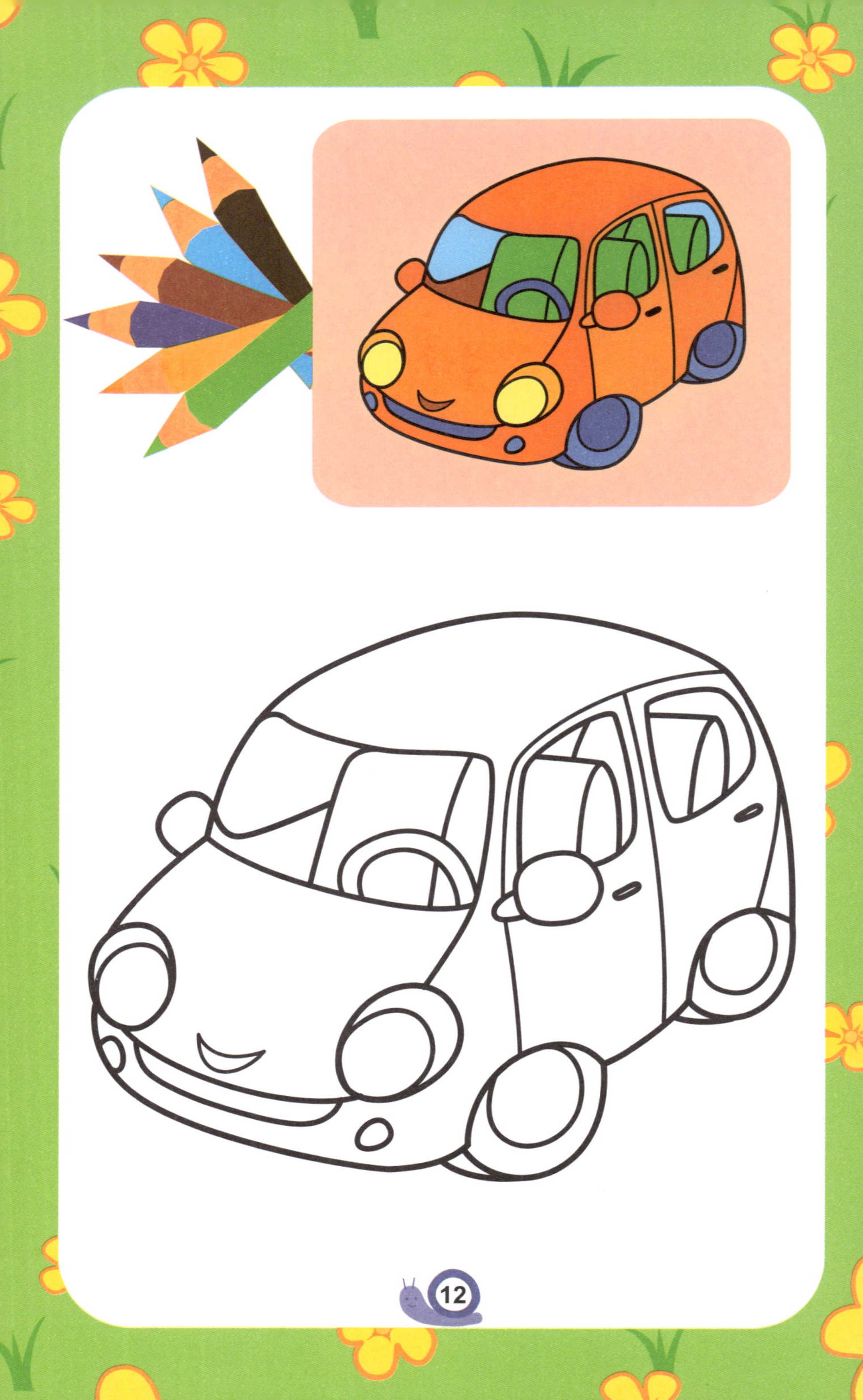

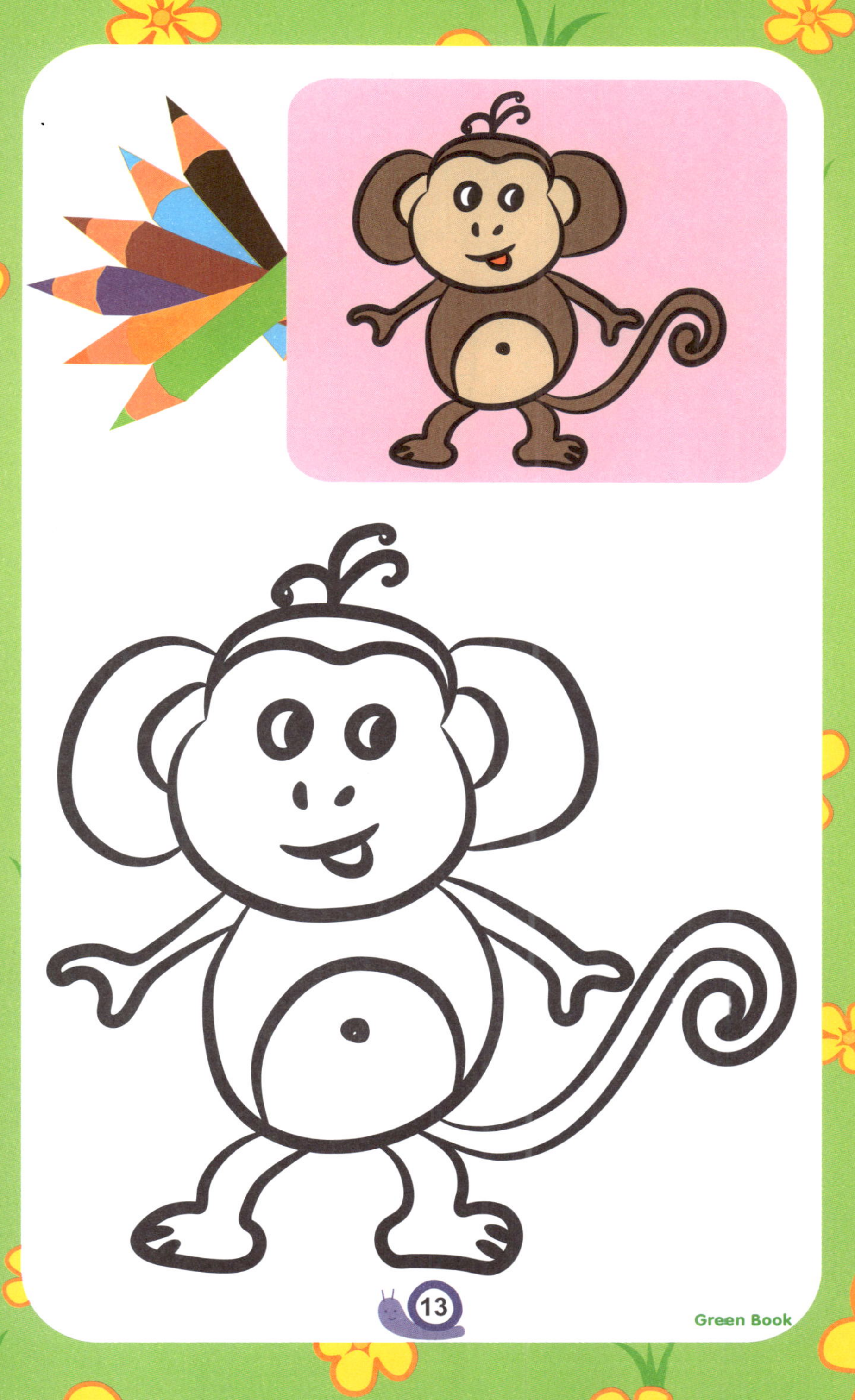

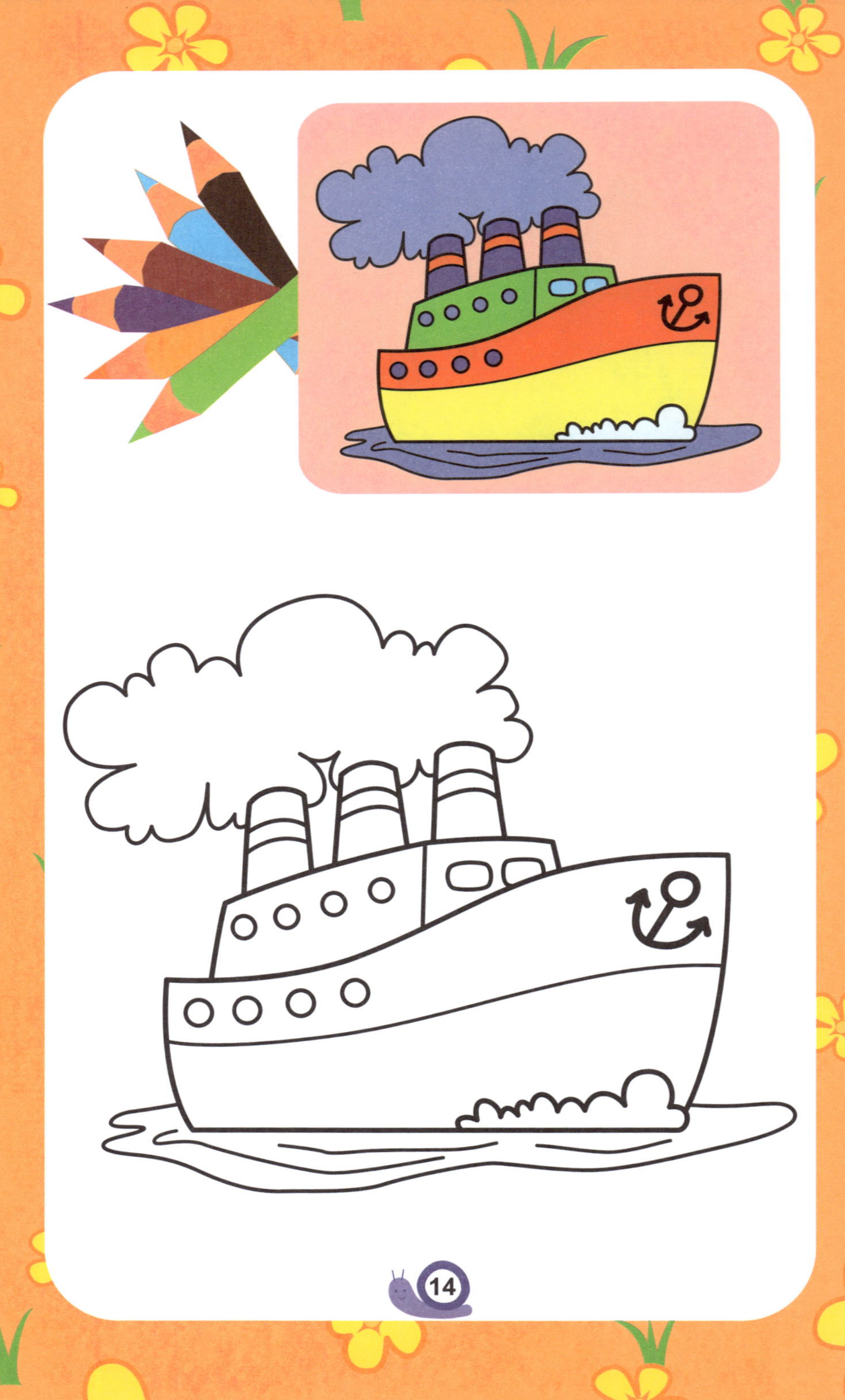

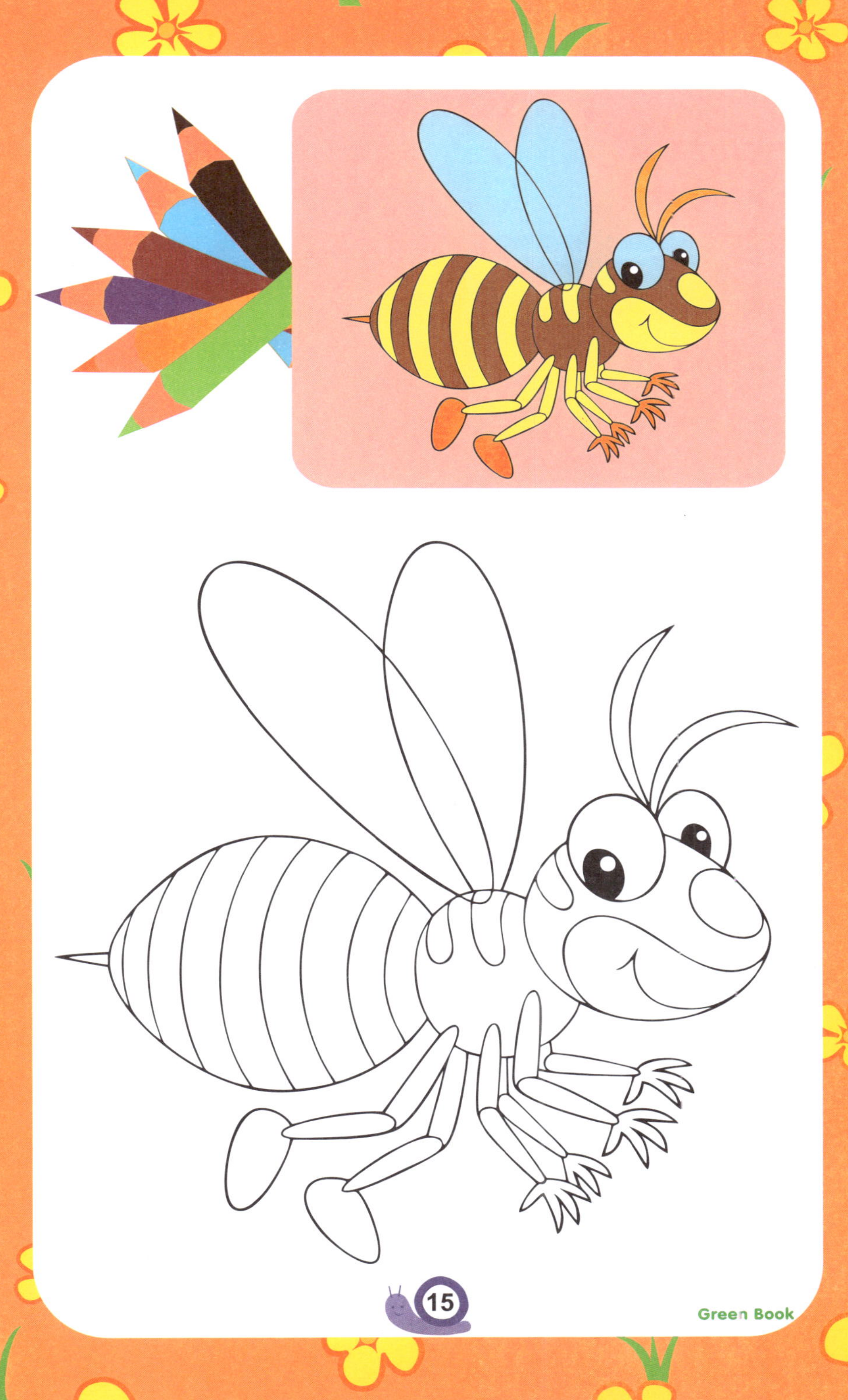

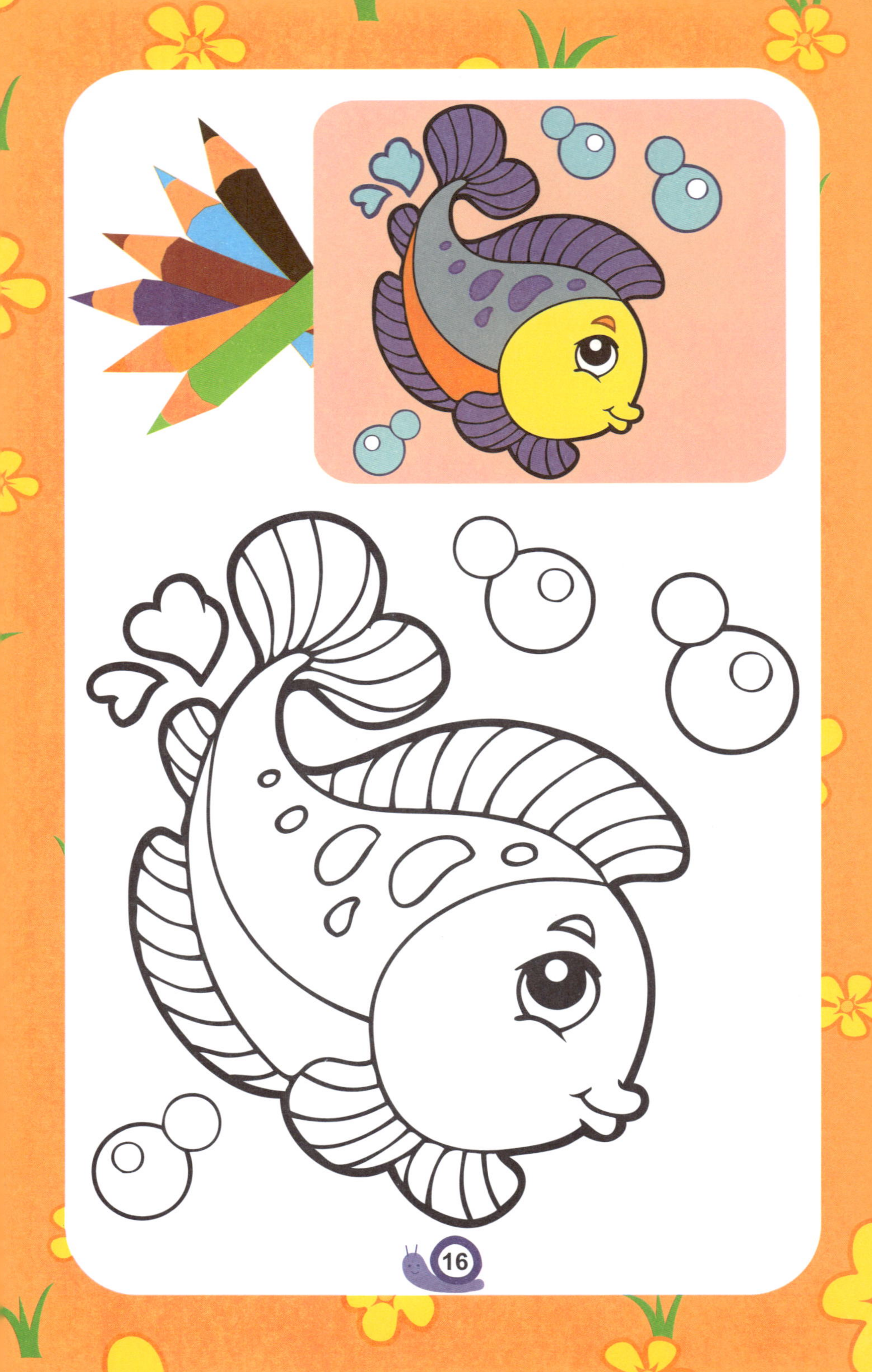